UNLOCKING YOU

UNLOCKING YOU

QUENTIN GRZYB

GRZYB BOOKS

GRZYB BOOKS

1 3 5 7 9 10 8 6 4 2

All poems copyright © Quentin Grzyb 2020
Publication copyright © Quentin Grzyb 2020

The right of Quentin Grzyb to be identified as the author of this Work has been asserted by them in accordance with the Copyright, Designs and Patents Act 1988

All rights reserved

First published in 2020 by
Grzyb Books

ISBN 978 0 9999013 7 3

This publication may not be used, reproduced, stored or transmitted in any way, in whole or in part, without the express written permission of the author. Nor may it be otherwise circulated in any form of binding or cover other than that in which it has been published and without a similar condition imposed on subsequent users or purchasers.

All characters in this publication are fictitious and any similarity to real persons, alive or dead, is coincidental.

Contents

Introduction	i
Redemption is Mine	1
Hope in Darkness	2
Seeing is not Believing	3
Unspoken Truth	4
Fail Forward Not Back	5
Living Your Dream	6
Coming Out	7
Commit to Change	8
Greatness	9
Faith	10
Mind of A Champion	11
Unlocking Each Other	12
Holding onto The Past	13
Spiritual Faith	14
Don't Screw It Up	15
Hands Up	16
A Gift for All	17
Change by Failure	18
The Ugly Truth	19
I Say "Rise"	20
Moving Forward	21
The Inevitable	22
Be Yourself	23
Fear Me Not	24
The Journey	25
Stepping Up	26
Life Through the Light	27
Time Alone	28
Anxiety	29
Hustle & Grind	30
Reasons of Pain	31
Unforgivable	32
Knowledge Bank	33
Why Change	34
Fall Hard	35
Nine to Five	36
Natural Selection	37
Fallen Society	38
Prayer to God	39
Blessings	40
The Truth Behind It All	41
COVID-19	42
The Awakening	43

Introduction

Everyone possesses an innate gift making us individually truly distinctive. We all want to achieve something far greater from within, and that is to become our very best. I want you to disregard what you have learned about yourself and revamp your image. Your newfound sense of motivation will reinforce your journey to success. We have followed society's foundation of success but not for long. What you see is what you get. It's time for you to take risks. Always aim to become your best not to become the one ahead of you.

Redemption is Mine

From childhood, I have suffered
As an adult, my heart is fractured
My past life makes me feel tortured
Why must I relive this to feel captured

Despite my success, I must regret
Because of my parents, I lost respect
God tells his children to forgive and forget
Now is the time to come to parents and confess

I go to church to say my prayers
That one day, I will confront my father
You say I am dead to you, but I am a fighter
There is nowhere to hide but to face the answers

Now mom, don't be afraid
I see through all your pain
The path ahead is straight
I will guide you all the way

For all these years, I lived in stress
With God, my self-confidence is fearless
My life now is filled with love and centeredness
I have established my obligations and successfulness.

Hope in Darkness

Being face to face with hostility is a challenge
You can either try to resolve it or retreat from it
What is worse is that you can't do each of them
Either decision alone will end up being the same

I can see your pain in your eyes
The feeling of guilt and trapped
All you want in the end is peace
But you can't achieve it anyway

With heavy heart, there is much confusion
Am I making the right or wrong decision
Sometimes, I wish I can just get lost
To be alone and seek direction

Emotionally, I am connected
Physically, I am disconnected
My heart can't take it anymore
Despite my reality, there is good

I know that it is a long shot
I hope that life will get better
In due time, everything will heal
Persistence and positivity are there.

Seeing is not Believing

Seek not what you see
Open your heart to the truth
The answer is there.

Unspoken Truth

An open mind is a book where the contents are truths
Some of us are afraid to come into facing with them
Our insecurities become the walls of ignorant pride
Ending in our demise where we fail to see the end

There is light at the end of every truth
The truth is, are we ready to face the light
Eventually, our conscience catches up with us
Through clarity, we can accept that change is now

Be open with yourself
Vulnerable isn't weakness
Humility teaches us of wisdom
No one can't change you except you.

Fail Forward Not Back

There will be times when you'll fall
What you see as failure can rise up
Your ability to push through is there
You must have the courage to face it

Faith will be your guide
All you have to do is believe
The answer you seek will come
The challenges will become simple

With struggle comes endurance
That will take you very far ahead
The heart, mind, and soul as one
The will to carry on fuels the spirit

Move forward not backwards
Nothing can't stop you except you
Take a deep breath and be prepared
Your next move will make a difference now.

Living Your Dream

How many of you dream?
How many of them come true?
What you desire comes from the heart
Ask yourself this, "What will you do to get it?"

You are a slave to society
You allow them to dictate you
When will you see past the facade
Your dream to aspire is just a step away

Your lifestyle and dream have a wall
Will power will propel you to remove it
Freeing what you dreamed of into reality
Release your restraints and live what you love

The moment your dream is within sight
You will feel complete and in control of life
You have lived for yourself and your ambitions
Life is beautiful so live it to the fullest and smile.

Coming Out

You've lived in silence
This is your time to speak out
Show them who you are.

Commit to Change

Achieving is to go above and beyond
What you desire must be attainable
You must be comfortable anyplace
If it means feeling uncomfortable

It is okay to scared and confident
To be scared is an act of normalcy
To overcome fear betters oneself
This is a challenge we face now

We all have ambitions within us
The question is, "what will you do?"
Through hardship, one can understand
Your drive to success is driven by your desire

If you want achieve then do something different
Commit yourself to achieving to what is a necessity
Be real and honest within and make moves that matter
Only then you will achieve what you desire and look higher.

Greatness

Gather yourself day by day
Remember what's important
Elaborate on your obligations
Acknowledge your necessities
Treat life with love and respect
New changes manifests visions
Envision a brighter future ahead
Seize your moment and be ready
Success by patience is obtainable.

Faith

Love with all your soul
Separate Earth from Heaven
We praise in his name.

Mind of A Champion

Embrace who you are
Defeat give rise to success
Self-motivation.

Unlocking Each Other

We are at our happiest when we are complete
The potential that is from within can be unlocked
By seeking the key element that affiliates our need
The riddle to this can be discovered by us opening up

I want you to look at yourself
What are you missing in your life
What fuels your vision to be fulfilled?
It is a common goal that we all look for

What we lack in weakness
Our counterpart can strengthen
It's obvious and it's staring right at you
What makes you strong is your partnership

The beauty in all of this is unique
What you admire is different per person
Your relationship to whom you admire is special
They will unlock your hidden ability to become the best

It is a journey in life best traveled
In the brightest and darkest of times
No matter what happens, you have them
Your internal accomplishments are their external.

Holding onto The Past

We all don't like to admit it
Our past defines who we are today
I am not proud of my past, but I accept it
My past can be described as a war of depression

My character is based upon my parents
My father wasn't much of an influence to me
My mother was absent in my life hidden in the dark
I was removed and coped in an environment of discomfort

My life was never the same
I didn't have much of a childhood
Living inside a strict family household
Survival was all I knew and had to depend on

Freedom allowed me to access my potential
Using my acquired knowledge, I executed plans
Looking for the right time to strike with my opinions
I know that it's unacceptable for what I am about to commit

Honesty is the best policy
I had to be honest to myself
My family had its own agenda
I marched on my path to freedom

Adulthood is filled with expectations
I was shielded from them because I allowed it
I suffered many disappointments on both sides of me
I learned that the world around me was all a lie in disguise

My adulthood derives from my youth
I lacked social compliancy due to my family
I have lost much but gained knowledge in return
Freedom has set me from free my chains but not my past.

Spiritual Faith

Many of us struggle
Struggle with our finances
We are insecure within ourselves
Without faith, we lose sight of freedom

Through faith, we will be free
You can't be enslaved to money
While having faith with God himself
Money can never fulfill our souls but God

You can't hold onto earthly assets
What God has for you has more value
By God's grace, you shall feel no shame
Financially faith brings glory to happiness

Be faithful to God's blessing
Appreciate what you're given
Give your tenth; it shall multiply
Financial freedom is through faith.

Don't Screw It Up

The world we live in is delusional
Where everything is fun and games
When our outcomes become our reality,
We begin to go into denial and can't face it

We can't play games
The life we're given is limited
One choice can make a difference
You have to take control of your life now

You must tell yourself the honest truth
Am I going to blame everyone for my faults?
The answer to that is quite obvious; you're to blame
If you want to make difference, you have to be accountable

What you decide as of now
Will make a difference in the future
What I can say is this, "better think twice"
You never know if you will live another or pass on.

Hands Up

When faced with a life-threatening situation,
One must take into account who is involved in it
The subconscious mind triggers your flight or fight
In that moment, you would have to make that decision

Protection is important to family
You protect those who you love
Placing your life in front of them
Fear manifests your motivation

Danger is in every corner
Alertness is your survival
Protection is contingency
Don't be afraid of anyone.

A Gift for All

You have a gift
A gift that is unique
Something to be shared
A natural position bestowed

You can change the world
You might ask yourself how
The answer is quite simplistic
What you seek is within yourself

Your ability to influence has impact
The outcome of your future starts here
This is the gift that has been given to you
Apply what is in you and become your best

To change the world, you must change yourself
How you envision the future is your infrastructure
Plan with commitment and actual goals for success
The world is yours as your gift is your tool, use it wisely.

Change by Failure

Don't expect to change
If you're heart isn't pure
You must lose yourself.

The Ugly Truth

When faced with yourself
You become more aware of you
What you do and say make an impact
When you become your enemy, it's hurtful

Every action produces a reaction
You're the product of your own action
Open your mind to what you are blinded
Is what you do even worth it without thinking

The ones closest to you will disappear
You are as good as those in your circle
Your Environment is your own stupidity
Open your mind and speak with a heart

We become victims to ourselves
I am my own enemy to everyone
It's time to stop the insensitivity
It's not worth losing everything.

I Say "Rise"

Get up
Yeah you
Get up now
You can do it

I know life can be hard
It's time for you to suck it up
You will always be knocked down
So, get use to reality and face the truth

The truth is, we are told one thing
"Trust in those who are closest to you"
This saying is applicable most of the time
Otherwise, you'll be stab in the back most likely

I want you to look into a mirror
What you see is a false perception
Underneath all of that is your foundation
Change your foundation by removing yourself

Reinvent yourself
What's your core value
Trust in yourself to elevate
What you become is your action.

Moving Forward

As this year comes to an end,
We give thanks to the new year
Our past becomes our reflection
Allowing us to review our moments

There's beauty in this celebration
Preparing a clean slate at midnight
Counting down to the last final hours
We say farewell as we are saying hello

There is no greater joy than this
As we raise our glasses and shout
Voices rising during the countdown
The lights getting brighter at the end

The ball drops with amazement
Everyone explodes with excitement
We cheer as the new year is finally here
What was a thing of past is now brand new

Congratulations to you all
Raise your glasses with a toast
For this is a new start to a new end
Enjoy your life with a Happy New Year!

The Inevitable

There comes a moment when we must face the light
Yes, that light, the one at the end of the tunnel we call life
Most of us dread, fear, and dislike the ideology in our minds
The truth is we must come to grips, before we rise into the sky

Planning for the future requires precision
We must be methodical with each decision
What we do now is a contribution to our vision
Our dedication will bring rise to a new generation

Humanity doesn't exist to live forever
Stop living a lie and become an influencer
Make the right decisions for a life that's brighter
Embrace the life you have now and become stronger.

Be Yourself

Stop proving yourself to everyone
Despite what others may think of you,
You can change yourself instead for them

If you have a problem, you have to look inside
No one can solve your issues so stop looking to them
Sometimes, you have to be by yourself than around others

If you seek what you want, then you will see
You can follow others or you can lead your own path
Be yourself and make the change for the very right reasons

You will always be knocked down, deal with it
It may hurt now, but you will learn and adjust then
Time will heal all pain but it does not forget it, that's a fact

A word to the wise, "Look into a mirror"
Begin to know your deepest regrets, don't hide it
Embrace yourself and dedicate your life to actual change

Life, in general, is not perfect
Your ups and downs don't define you
You have a choice, be someone else or be real.

Fear Me Not

It's okay to feel afraid
It's not okay to ignore it
What we fear controls us
This becomes an epidemic

Many of us go about our lives
As we live life, we conceal our fears
Some of us are afraid to express them
Through courage, we can learn about fear

Your fear can either make you or break you
You can stay where you are at in life or change it
Fear is nothing more than an obstacle to be overcome
The more confidence you have the stronger you become

It's easy to lose yourself by what you fear
It is another to feel in control of your own life
Don't be afraid to embrace what you fear within
As what you are afraid of will give you your strength

To fear is to be human
Recognize your capability
Only you can break this cycle
Take your courage, fear no more.

The Journey

What you love inside your heart defines who you are
It doesn't matter what anybody says here and now
If you believe in change, then change is possible
Many will try to test your limits but don't worry
Your will to succeed will conquer obstacles
You must envision yourself in your future

What you love and desire are different
Your love is driven by your emotion
What you desire is manipulated
Stop listening to your reality
Define what's truly ideal
Your journey is yours.

Stepping Up

Deep in our subconscious minds,
There is a secret that lies behind

We have a tendency to believe
That right there is a false belief

Through self-discovery, you'll see
What your potential future can be

Take action and make a decision
Anything is attainable with precision

Always put yourself first in your life
What makes you happy feels right

Now that you have a new perspective,
The goals you seek must be productive

You are in control of your actions
Be the reason of positive attraction.

Life Through the Light

Dear self, how are you
I know life has changed you
All I want to tell you is to be true

Life can be hard but beautiful
At times, you can feel like a fool
Overall, the outcome is wonderful

The most successful may struggle
You have to think smart and humble
Words to the wise, keep your head up

You and I have come a long way
So never forget to look up and pray
Everything you have seen is portrayed

Deep down inside if you feel nervous
Just remember, you live for a purpose
By his guidance, you'll see the surface.

Time Alone

Deep down, I am lonely
Always feeling empty
Secretly inside I cry
I keep asking, why

Physically, I am broken
Mentally, my mind has spoken
Psychologically, I am a dysfunction
My life can best be defined a depression

Time and time again, I fail
Many don't know, my soul is frail
History repeats just like my mistakes
This feeling inside my heart always aches

I know with time comes healing
I can only pray and hope to be freed
I know this life is hard and it be very steep
Through my confidence I can achieve anything.

Anxiety

Once in a while, we become afraid
When faced with realty, we run away
One moment our thoughts become gray

It can be hard to be brave
Our fears begin to cultivate
False truths start to manipulate

The truth is we face anxiety
That is most of our reality
It affects our insecurity

Anxiety will never leave
It blocks us to achieve
We succumb to belief

Every day, I ask myself why
For my sanity, I must comply
Anxiety is a poison in my mind.

Hustle & Grind

As the door clicks open,
The cold fresh air hits me
The smell of new equipment
Reminding me where I feel free

I close my eyes and open my mind
Where my goals and ambitions lie
I open my eyes to see my motivation
I know who I am and what I have to do

As I glide my hand across the bar,
A surge of energy flows through me
Gripping the cold steel with my hands,
The energy within manifesting into a lift

With each lift, my motivation grows
Nothing can't stop me not even pain
It is my ambition within that drives me
My arms and chest fibers ripping apart

There is no greater feeling than this
Cold sweat flowing down my wet face
With each set performed to a perfection
Without dedication, there is no achievement.

Reasons of Pain

I can't take back what I have done
I must face reality that I am to blame
I can't fix the pain which I have caused
What I can do is accept and move forward

I am ashamed of what I have become
With my shame comes humility and guilt
I have grown in the past days to hate myself
This internal hatred now consumes me mentally

It pains me to see others suffer because of me
Only to me see me as their common denominator
I ask myself why must I place myself in these dilemmas
I cry myself into agony forever tortured by my own disgust

I don't wish to continue my madness
I wish to seek peace and a resolution
I want to be able to heal those near me
Lastly, I want to escape it and be renewed

I have prayed to God
Asking each and every day
For his grace and his guidance
All I want is to make a difference

We all stray away, it is human nature
In the end, we all can change if we want
I have come face to face with my humiliations
I can't change my past, but I can seek redemption.

Unforgivable

I stand here staring at the fragments of myself
I'm scared to take a step because it hurts so much
What was once complete now is shattered into pieces
I do not know what to think from here except eternal pain

I have done the unspeakable
My action can't be forgiven; I did it
The shame itself makes me go into silence
I have cried from within; until I can't look at myself

Each time, it is spoken; I have fallen into a depression
I am trapped in an endless loop forever tormented again
I can't turn back the hands of time only to face my demon
I don't foresee forgiveness any time soon as I'm depressed

Life is hard but I must face the truth
If I want to be forgiven, I must act now
To conquer my demon, I will have face it
I can't be a disappointment to those I love.

Knowledge Bank

Wisdom teaches us many things of life
From how we socially interact with people
To how we conduct ourselves in our daily lives
In the end, it is the wisdom transferred down onto us

Wisdom is an encyclopedia of knowledge
Knowledge that acknowledges morals and ethics
This in turn creates an intellectual individual to a society
The more we become appreciative of wisdom, the better we get

Not everyone will know better
You can change yourself not others
Unfortunately, with wisdom comes failure
That is how wisdom can be obtained eventually

Despite this fact, wisdom do come with age
Some learn quickly; others it takes more time
Nonetheless, wisdom has patience for everyone
We must not allow our ignorance to create a wall

By sharing our knowledge, we share wisdom
The minds of the uneducated becomes more educated
Slowly and surely, we will all become wiser as a society
So, open your mind as the knowledge you gain is a blessing.

Why Change

Mentally, we tell ourselves that we will change
Despite all the talk behind it, how many of it is true?
We can try to fool ourselves by telling us that, I will do it
Only to fail most of the time therefore starting all over again

This is a struggle I share from within
Though I'm not perfect, I am still trying
I have to remind myself why I am changing
Then, I will then find my true sense of direction

I will admit that change is difficult
Some of us have a hard time with it
I tell myself that I'll change my habits
Only to find myself falling back on them

We have to be careful with our emotions
Some changes can affect how we feel inside
The motives of our changes are our own reflection
How do I know this, I am victim of my emotional stress?

Despite how change can affect us all there's hope
I do believe that with the right mindset it is possible
We can't allow ourselves to fall into an endless cycle
On the contrary, those of us who struggle can change

Change is more than just a promise
Change has to have a sense of direction
Our minds must be disciplined to be focused
From that point, then we can change our pursuit.

Fall Hard

Success isn't perfect
Failures allows improvements
Fall hard fall forward.

Nine to Five

The average lifespan is short, why?
It's because we focus more on work
Many of us don't know how to live life
We're brainwashed that work is happy

Working nine to five is a struggle
We are miserable with our careers
To the average person, work is to live
To live one must work to receive money

Here is the truth ladies and gentlemen
Working all day shortens your lifespan
Working over living actually is stressful
Most importantly, money isn't happiness

This misconception affects how we live
Life is not all about working day in and out
Life is the balance of our mental and physical
So, ask yourself, "Do I work to live or live to work?"

Natural Selection

Many of us come from a time when we struggled
Nowadays, we either make it out or remain trapped
Success changes people for the greater or for worse
Sometimes, we forget who we are and where we came

When one makes it out, the person wants even more
We tend to focus on acquiring what we never had before
We change from within; therefore, we change our character
Change is good from time to time, but it too can be even toxic

Being humble teaches us to appreciate everything
Through change, we must remember our inner roots
What was taught to us is meant to evolve even further
For true change to occur, one must differentiate morality.

Fallen Society

Our daily lives are shaped by our social environment
Our inner circle defines how we interact with each other
Though this is a benefit to many of us; it is a major downfall

Communication is a critical requirement for our sanity
Prior to technology, we used to communicate in person
Now, our faces are in our phones speaking through video

Before there was social hierarchy, there was respect
People actually greeted one another, now they're silent
What ever happened to human common sense these days?

Social in general is a friendly conversation
Social by society is to post nonsense gossip
Socialization is meant to be in face and formal

How we see life and speak of it will differ
How we view the average norm is up to you
Having proper respect and hospitality matters.

Prayer to God

In times of desperation,
I fear for our fallen nation
Protect us from this dire time
As our faith is becoming blind

Some of us tainted see only evil
By you, we can end this upheaval
Our mortal reality is but temporary
What you have planned is for glory

Though our final days ahead may be uncertain
We won't submit to fear due to of your instruction
This earthly realm on which I walk upon is by the devil
With you always on my heart and soul, the devil trembles

Consumed by our cruel reality
Society has replaced their sanity
Through faith, I know you are there
With a heavy heart, I say this prayer.

Blessings

I know life can be tough
Sometimes, it can be rough

Life isn't always going to be happy
Personally, you must to be stress free

We get comfortable, until it's all gone
The truth is we are in a game as pawns

Materialism actually has no real value
Your heart is richer and knows what's true

When a door closed another one opens
Always live your life filled with appreciation

What you are experiencing right now is fear
Before you know it, how you feel will disappear

Nothing is perfect nor last, let us be honest
What we will gain after will make us reflect.

The Truth Behind It All

Being famous comes with a price
With power requires a "sacrifice"
Becoming the status, we idolize
Thus, living to see our demise

Psychologically, we are blind
Our subconscious "compromised"
Reprogrammed to influence more lies
What was once human is no longer inside

Look into their eyes and what do you see
Another zombie "promoting" a social media scene
Society constantly scrolling down on posts like its candy
We have grown accustomed to what we call life, is this reality?

For once, let's think for ourselves
This is the time to realize and protect
Deep down you're "human", don't you forget
The more we expand our independence, we can live

You can't be naive to what is in front of you
You must separate the constant lies from the "truth"
We must protect the next generation of the upcoming youth
Our survival is in our ability to see past the darkness and seek virtue.

COVID-19

We believe in misconceptions
Day by day, our fear grows more
Solitary confinement in a pandemic
Not knowing what's to come, worrying

In times of crisis, we are divided
What was once socially acceptable
Now is forbidden thus seeming awkward
Though we live like prisoners, we are still free

In desperate times, you must be strong
Clear your conscience of all the distractions
Challenge yourself by seeking past your reasoning
Manipulation exists as to infect the mind with deception

Throw away what you have been told
Make your decisions and be conscience
The more you learn the more you will apply
For those who are oppressing become scared

You become what they fear the most
Leadership and intelligence are your weapon
This pandemic is a tactical attack of oppression
Be patient as your time will come to rise above those.

The Awakening

Far too long, our equality has endured injustice abuse
How can we receive justice, if we are faced with excuses?
We pray with faith in our system to find out that, it is useless
Despite peaceful protests, the senseless violence still continues

We exercise our constitutional rights
Yet police brutality makes us fear for our lives
Eventually, there will come a time when we must fight
Under desperation, we look to God so that our spirits rise

As children, we are taught to be brothers and sisters
Racists aren't born; instead, they're taught to hate others
Raised by God, the love within us is our greatest act of power
Satan is a conniving snake, we will not fall as we are our protector

If you don't know, death is not a choice
Let's join as one nation becoming one voice
When Satan's' reign comes to an end, we rejoice
We must continue to strive in the name of George Floyd.

Lightning Source UK Ltd.
Milton Keynes UK
UKHW020632171020
371758UK00009B/221